Kavya saanjh: A symphony of poems

Aradhana

BookLeaf Publishing

India | USA | UK

Presentation by *BookLeaf Publishing*

Web: www.bookleafpub.com

E-mail: info@bookleafpub.com

ISBN: 9789363311350

First edition 2024

Dedication

To my family,

For your endless love and unwavering support,

For nurturing my dreams and encouraging my spirit,

This collection is dedicated to you.

To my mother,

Whose strength, warmth, and wisdom light my way,

Your example has shaped my heart and guided my journey.

Thank you for teaching me the power of love and resilience.

And to all those who strive to live their truth,

May these words inspire and uplift,

And remind you that your light shines brightest

When you embrace who you truly are.

ACKNOWLEDGEMENT

Creating "Kavya Saanjh: A Symphony of Poems" has been a journey enriched by the love and support of many remarkable people. I am deeply grateful to everyone who has walked beside me throughout this creative endeavor.

To my family, thank you for your unwavering encouragement, understanding, and boundless love. Your belief in me has been my anchor and inspiration. To my mother, who embodies grace and resilience, your spirit infuses each word with warmth and strength.

To my friends, thank you for being my sounding board, offering insights and cheering me on every step of the way. Your thoughtful feedback helped shape this collection into what it is today.

To all my readers, thank you for joining me in this poetic journey. I hope these verses resonate with you, provide solace, and remind you of the importance of staying true to yourself.

Finally, to all poets and writers who have come before, your words have paved the way, lighting paths with your brilliance and inspiring countless voices, including mine. I am honored to share my work among such a luminous company.

With deepest gratitude,
Aradhana

PREFACE

In a land rich with tradition, stories, and rhythm, poetry often blooms like wildflowers—vibrant and diverse. This collection, "Kavya Saanjh: A Symphony of Poems," brings together verses that seek to echo the heartfelt whispers and vivid dreams that flow through the tapestry of life.

Inspired by the resilience and grace of everyday life, the words within these pages reflect a journey of being true to oneself and others. They delve into the warmth of family, the challenges of navigating modern life, and the enduring power of honesty. Each poem carries a note of reflection, hope, and wisdom drawn from the vibrant world around us and the rich heritage of Indian culture.

In this collection, you will find solace and inspiration, as these verses celebrate the spirit of authenticity amid all odds. May this book remind you that no matter the challenges life presents, staying true to your core values will always lead to fulfillment and peace.

Thank you for joining me on this poetic journey. I hope these poems resonate with you, stir your emotions, and offer comfort or insight whenever you turn to them.

With gratitude,
Aradhana

True to yourself

When life feels like it's closing in,
And makes you start to doubt,
Hold tight to who you really are,
Don't let that light burn out.

The world might tell you who to be,
Or try to change your mind,
But trust yourself and listen close,
Your truth is what you'll find.

When hard times come and make you think,
That bending would be best,
Stand tall and let your spirit shine,
You'll rise above the rest.

Sometimes it's tough to speak your truth,
When others walk away,
But know that you are strong enough,
To live your own true way.

Be kind to those who need a friend,
And kind to yourself too,
For in your heart, there's strength to grow,
No matter what you do.

So stay the course and hold on tight,
To all that's good and true,
For the greatest gift you can give the world,
Is simply being you.

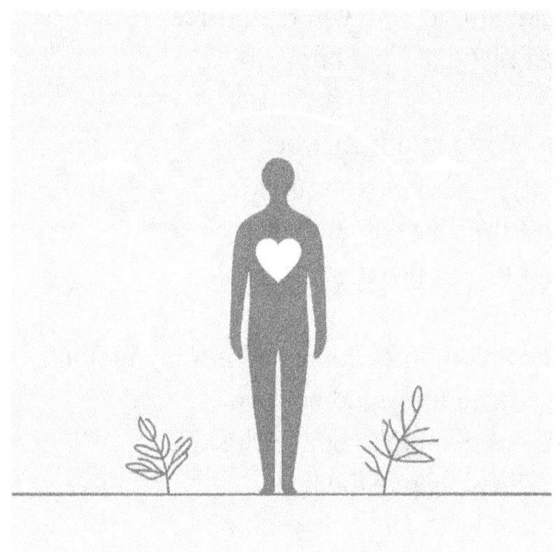

A Brighter Tomorrow

When morning comes with a soft glow,
And sunlight makes the shadows go,
I wake and smile, feeling light,
Ready to make the day feel bright.

A happy grin can travel far,
And lift us up, like rising stars.
With laughter flowing like a breeze,
We see the world with joyful ease.

When worries seem to block our way,
We find some hope to guide our day.
In every heart, let's plant a seed,
Of kindness, love, and all we need.

Each new challenge makes us strong,
With hopeful dreams to move along.
We face the storm without a tear,
With steady hearts and no more fear.

The road is long, but bright and clear,
When we hold hope and joy so dear.
For every day we look to find,
A light that lifts our weary mind.

With smiles shared and truth in sight,
We'll spread our joy both day and night.
With open hearts and eyes on high,
We'll lift each other to the sky.

So hold my hand, let's go explore,
With faith and courage, find much more.
Together strong, we'll see it through,
A brighter world awaits us too.

A Mother's Embrace

In the glow of morning's gentle light,
She rises from her rest,
To nurture all the dreams we hold,
Within her tender breast.

Her heart, a boundless ocean deep,
Where waves of love reside,
She grants each wish we softly whisper,
With joy she cannot hide.

A son she holds in steadfast arms,
Two daughters now take flight,
She celebrates their every step,
And anchors them each night.

In quiet grace, she weaves her magic,
Through every corner of our home,
A symphony of laughter fills,
The world she built alone.

Though days may dim and nights may tire,
Her spirit never wanes,
Each burden she shoulders silently,
No whisper of complaints.

For in her eyes, a universe,
Where warmth and solace blend,
A caring heart, a faithful friend,
Our truest guiding end.

A mother's love, a sacred bond,
No distance can undo,
We cherish you, our dearest one,
For everything you do.

A lifetime may not be enough,
To repay all you've given,
But know that you are treasured still,
And loved beyond the heavens.

Everlasting love: A journey together

In the dance of life, hand in hand,
Together we walk, a united band.
Through joys and sorrows, thick and thin,
Our love endures, a bond to win.

In your eyes, I find my home,
A place of solace, where I roam.
Your touch, a comfort, a soothing balm,
In your arms, I find my calm.

You are my rock, my guiding light,
In your presence, everything feels right.
Through every storm, we stand strong,
In each other's hearts, we belong.

We laugh together, we cry together,
In every moment, we're birds of a feather.
Our love story, a tale of two hearts,
Never to part, never to depart.

So here's to us, my love, my life,
Through all the struggles, all the strife.
In your love, I find my bliss,
Forever sealed with a tender kiss.

A father's love: A daughter's Grace

In a father's caring arms, a daughter finds peace,
His love for her will never cease.
He teaches her to be strong and brave,
Guiding her steps, her heart he'll save.

He's her hero, her guiding light,
In his presence, everything feels right.
He protects her from every harm,
In his embrace, she feels warm.

As she grows, their bond grows too,
In his eyes, she sees love so true.
He's her support, always there,
In his love, she finds solace rare.

Their bond is strong, it will never break,
A father's love, no one can fake.
In his love, she finds her place,
A father's love, a daughter's grace.

Daughter:My heart's song

In her eyes, I see the dawn of my days,
A daughter's love, in so many ways.
She's the light that brightens my darkest night,
My heart's delight, my soul's purest flight.

With every smile, she paints my world anew,
A rainbow of hope, in skies so blue.
Her laughter, a melody, so sweet and clear,
A symphony of joy, to my ears so dear.

She's the warmth in my coldest hour,
A gentle touch, like a blooming flower.
Her hugs, a haven, so safe and true,
In her embrace, all troubles subdue.

In her, I see a reflection of me,
A bond so strong, yet light and free.
She's my teacher, my guide, my muse,
In her innocence, my heart finds its fuse.

A daughter, a gift, a treasure untold,
A love so pure, a story unfolds.
In her, I find my purpose, my reason to be,
My daughter, my life, eternally.

Morning's embrace: A walk to wellness

"Morning's Embrace: A Walk to Wellness"

In the early light, before the world awakes,
A morning walk, the soul it shakes.
The air is crisp, the breeze is light,
A peaceful time, before the day's fight.

With every step, a new day starts,
A chance to heal our weary hearts.
The world is quiet, the mind is clear,
A time for reflection, far and near.

The benefits of a morning walk are many,
For body, mind, and soul, if any.
It wakes us up, gets us moving,
Sets the tone for the day, improving.

It strengthens the body, keeps it fit,
Improves our mood, gives us wit.
It clears the mind, reduces stress,
A simple practice, we must confess.

So let's embrace the morning's call,
And go for a walk, big or small.
For in those moments, so serene,
We find beauty in life's routine.

Life of a hawker

In the busy streets where people roam,
There stands a hawker, far from home.
His cart is filled with goods to sell,
A story of his life to tell.

From morning light till evening falls,
He calls out loud, his voice it calls.
Through heat and rain, he doesn't rest,
His spirit strong, he gives his best.

His wares are simple, his prices fair,
He sells with pride, he doesn't despair.
Each sale he makes, a small delight,
In his world, everything's just right.

He knows the streets, every turn and bend,
His daily path, from end to end.
His voice a melody in the air,
A song of life, beyond compare.

But in his heart, beneath the tough facade,
There lies a man, not just a facade.
For in his humble, everyday grind,
A kind and gentle soul, we find.

So let's remember, in our busy race,
The hawker's smile, his peaceful grace.
For in his simple, honest way,
He teaches us to live each day.

"From Dawn to Dusk: A Human's Journey Through Life"

Life of humans since childhood
From a tiny bud in nature's lap, life begins,
Growing with each passing day, learning life's hymns.
Childhood's joys, innocent and pure,
Exploring, discovering, life's allure.

Youth arrives, dreams take flight,
Passion and ambition burn bright.
Challenges come, tests to face,
Yet, with courage, we embrace.

Through life's seasons, we learn and grow,
Wisdom blooms, like a river's flow.
Family and friends, our guiding light,
Together, we face the darkest night.

As the years pass, and we grow old,
Memories cherished, like precious gold.
In the end, a life well-spent,
A journey of love, a testament.

"Truth's Echoes: A Poem on Honesty"

In the heart's quiet, where truth resides,
Honesty dwells, in soft, gentle tides.
It's a promise kept, a word well-spoken,
A bond of trust, never to be broken.

Like a warm hug, it comforts and cheers,
Wiping away doubt, calming all fears.
It's the smile of a friend, the hand that's true,
In honesty, we find our strongest glue.

No need for grand tales or fancy art,
Honesty shines in the simplest heart.
It's a clear mirror reflecting our best,
A guide through life's confusing test.

So let's cherish honesty, in word and in deed,
For it's the friend we all desperately need.
In its embrace, we find peace and light,
A beacon of truth, shining ever bright.

My days in court

Every day, I step into the court,
Where justice lives, and stories are short.
I've been here since 2003,
Seeing all there is to see.

The papers pile high on my desk,
And every case is like a test.
I've faced warnings that make me doubt,
But helping people is what it's about.

Sometimes, I'm really tired, my feet drag on the
floor,
But then someone smiles, and I remember what
I'm here for.
This job is tough, the days can be rough,
But it's in these moments, I've got to be tough.

The faces change, but the stories stick,
Some are hopeful, others tragic and quick.
In these walls, I've laughed and I've cried,
Felt the heartache when justice is denied.

Here, where right meets wrong,
I've found where I belong.
Each file, each law that comes my way,

I handle with care, come what may.

As the years pass, and I keep going,
My place in these halls keeps on growing.
I'm here to help, to do what's right,
In the heart of the court, from morning till night.

When machines take over

Machines are working day and night,
In places where bulbs are always bright.
They do things that humans used to do,
Making everything look shiny and new.

Where there used to be laughter and talk,
Now there's just the machines that walk.
They don't get tired, they don't need breaks,
But can they share our joys and aches?

Offices are quiet, just the sound of keys,
Machines work fast, with such ease.
They think and write, but can they feel?
Or understand what makes us real?

Machines don't dream or hope or care,
They don't know how to be fair or share.
They do their jobs without a mistake,
But they don't love, they don't ache.

We made these machines, to help, not replace,
To make life easier, not to erase.
But as they take over, what's left for us?
Are we just old parts collecting dust?

So, I wonder, as they do more,
What are we, the humans, really here for?
Machines might work better, faster, strong,
But they can't replace where we belong.

Life's messy, full of ups and downs,
Filled with smiles, sometimes frowns.
Machines might help, but they can't see
What it really means to be alive like you and me.

Brother far away

Thirty-five years, side by side,
Laughter shared and tears we've cried.
Now miles stretch between us wide,
But brother, you're still my pride.

Your new journey, under distant skies,
While here, our childhood playground lies.
Though oceans apart, our hearts entwine,
Your voice across the line, a lifeline fine.

Fly high and chase your dreams so bold,
In my heart, your story's told.
Always remember, no matter the place,
You're part of me, across time and space.

"Bonds of Love: A Poem on Family Ties"

In this world that's always changing,
Where dreams and paths can stray,
There's a place where love stays steady,
And never fades away.

A mother's hug, a father's smile,
A sibling's joyful cheer,
A gentle touch that holds us close,
And chases every fear.

Though roads may wind and miles may part,
And time may wear us down,
Family's love will pull us near,
And make us feel safe and sound.

We gather through our ups and downs,
And share each joy and fall,
Together, we are always strong,
United, one and all.

So here's to ties that hold us close,
A love that will not bend,
For family means everything,
Our first and truest friends.

Everything will be ok

In the quiet stillness of a star-filled night,
When the world feels heavy and nothing seems
right,
A gentle voice whispers to soothe your fear,
"Hold on, dear heart, the dawn is near."

Morning will come and bring its golden glow,
Washing away all the sorrow you know.
The storms will pass, and the skies will clear,
Making space for the joy that draws near.

In the garden where dreams are sown with care,
Delicate flowers blossom everywhere.
Petals soft and bright in a vibrant hue,
Turn toward the light, just like you.

In every heartbeat and every song,
A gentle rhythm says, "Stay strong."
The tides will calm, the waves will subside,
As courage and hope flow like the tide.

Through the tangled paths and winding ways,
Believe that light will find your days.
The burdens that weigh on your weary mind
Will ease with the peace you're sure to find.

So when shadows stretch and the night feels
long,
Remember the tune of that timeless song—
That time will heal, and sorrow will fade,
Leaving room for brighter memories made.

Trust that you hold the spark of grace,
To light your path and find your place.
In your darkest hour, seek out the bright,
For everything will be okay—hold tight.

"Forever in My Heart: A Poem for My Son"

Your tiny hands, your smile so bright,
My world is lit by your gentle light.
With each laugh and every cheer,
You fill my heart, my precious dear.

Your toddling steps across the floor,
Open wide my heart's door.
Your giggles echo, sweet and true,
There's nothing I won't do for you.

You paint my world with magic hues,
Every day brings something new.
The wonder in your sparkling eyes,
Is my morning sun, my starry skies.

Your curious gaze, your endless "why,"
Makes me marvel as the days go by.
Your joy and spirit light the way,
Brightening even the cloudiest day.

My love for you knows no end,
It's in every game of make-pretend.
In every hug and sleepy night,
In every wish for your dreams so bright.

So, my dear child, as you grow,
There's one thing I want you to know:
You'll always have my endless love,
My gift to you from up above.

My unfinished dream

In the glow of vows, we danced as one,
With dreams entwined and hopes begun.
He knew my heart, my spirit's flame,
The goals I held, my every aim.

But soon the promises broke apart,
My wings were clipped, it crushed my heart.
A love once bright, now cast in chains,
My laughter lost to endless pains.

No longer could I wear my grace,
Or choose my path or my embrace.
Dreams stifled by the weight of rules,
In halls of silence, love grew cruel.

Now, at forty-two, the years have flown,
And in my soul, the ache has grown.
The dreams I had to study more,
To learn, to grow, and so explore,

Lie buried deep, but never fade,
The light they held forever stayed.
A bitter truth that still remains,
Of how love's promises brought pains.

Yet, I hold tight to my inner light,
The spark that guides me through the night.
Though doors were closed and freedom lost,
My spirit burns despite the cost.

And though the world has held me still,
I'll rise again with iron will.
The dreams denied may never rest,
Their echoes live within my chest.

For now, I wear my battle scars,
And hold my dreams among the stars.
A warrior of my spirit's song,
I'm bound to dreams where I belong.

"Joyful Habits: Embracing the Happiness Within"

In the morning light, dreams come true,
One step at a time, joy shines through.
A bit of peace with every new day,
A positive start helps worries stay away.

Gratitude brightens the day's first glow,
Writing our thanks makes our smiles grow.
Meditation breathes with every sigh,
Stretching the body and letting it fly.

Movement brings us energy and fun,
Walk, dance, or play under the sun.
Exercise wakes up joy from within,

Lifting our mood, bringing a grin.

Healthy meals that are made with love,
Feed our souls and lift us above.
Laughter and warmth in every bite,
Filling our hearts with pure delight.

Mindfulness blooms in every breath,
Letting go of worries and stress.
Observe the moment and take your time,
Finding joy in each thought and rhyme.

Gratitude and kindness shape our day,
Sharing good deeds in all that we say.
Helping others spreads joy around,
Making happiness truly profound.

Friendships grow and bonds are strong,
In laughter and care, we all belong.
Family and friends stay close and near,
Bringing us comfort and calming our fear.

Our spaces are calm, neat, and bright,
Filled with things that bring us light.
Corners where peace and love can show,
A cozy home where joy will flow.

Daily goals that are clear and kind,
Create the happiness we want to find.

Fun hobbies, learning, and kindness, too,
Bring smiles and laughter all day through.

So, let's walk this journey with hearts full of
bliss,
Finding joy in the morning's sweet kiss.
Let daily habits build us a cheer,
And make the world a place we hold dear.

A mother's dream

I see you there, my lovely child,
Resting in your world so mild.
Your laughter fills the quiet air,
But deep inside, I hold a prayer.

I dream of paths you've yet to take,
Of goals achieved for your own sake.
Though books seem dull, your thoughts may
stray,
I believe in you, come what may.

I hope you'll see the dreams I hold,
How learning's worth more than gold.
Not just in marks or a fancy score,
But in the doors that knowledge opens more.

Your spirit shines in all you do,
I only wish you'd see it too.
That effort now, with care and grace,
Will lead to joy in every place.

So listen, dear, and hear my plea,
I'm not your judge, but a guide to be.
To help you find the joy within,
To chase your goals and see them win.

Rest, my child, and eat your fill,
But try the books with an open will.
One step each day, no rush, no race,
And together, we'll find your pace.

I love you deeply, this much is true,
My hopes are bright because of you.
For now, I wait, and dream, and pray,
That you'll find your path, in your own way.

"Letting Go: A Poem of Release"

Fourteen years of marriage strong,
A journey where I've walked along.
Yet, one day my feet were burned so deep,
Left to heal alone, with pain to keep.

No caring hands, no soothing voice,
My heart ached without a choice.
In that moment, I felt betrayed,
The wound still fresh, my trust decayed.

Now, X needs aid,
The same burden that on me was laid.

Y asks for my care,
A chance for compassion I'm called to share.

Though the scars still whisper of old pain,
I seek to let go, to love again.
To free my spirit and cleanse my mind,
To rise above, to be gentle and kind.

I offer solace, with a softened heart,
To help her heal and do my part.
For in forgiveness, I find my peace,
A weight released, the old wounds cease.

I choose the path that brings me light,
To mend the past, to do what's right.
To let go of hurt and hold on to grace,
To cherish each moment in this sacred space.

"Simple Joys: The True Wealth"

Happiness isn't found in a store,
It doesn't come from having more.
It's in the morning sun's first light,
In peaceful walks and quiet nights.

It lives in laughter, loud and free,
In the shade of an old oak tree.
In stories told, in jokes we share,
In the comfort of a friend who cares.

It's in warm hugs and smiles that glow,
In every place that feels like home.

In simple meals, in songs sung true,
In every old thing made anew.

Money buys things, that's all it does,
But happiness comes from what always was—
In every small, ordinary thing,
That's where happiness spreads its wings.

Joyful Moments

In the sparkle of eyes so bright,
Laughter fills the air tonight.
Hands clapping, feet dancing free,
Moments of joy, for you and me.

Balloons rise high, colors of glee,
Songs sung loud, in harmony.
Candles flicker on a cake so sweet,
Celebrations when we meet.

Together we share this time so rare,
In every smile, a love we declare.
For in these moments, hearts are light,
Everything feels just right.

So here's to joy, to love, to friends,
To all the good that never ends.
Let's hold these moments, keep them near,
Cherish them throughout the year.

Nature's Embrace

Outside my window, the world awakes,
Birds sing their songs, the morning breaks.
Green leaves shimmer with dewy glow,
Nature's beauty, a constant show.

Mountains stand with ancient grace,
Rivers run a never-ending race.
Flowers bloom in colors bold,
Stories of the earth, silently told.

Sunsets paint the sky in hues,
Pinks and oranges, purples and blues.
Stars twinkle in the quiet night,
Nature's wonder, pure delight.

In every breath, the wind's soft call,
Reminds us to embrace it all.
For in nature's arms, we find our peace,
In its beauty, a sweet release.

Light Through the Cracks

When days are dark and nights stretch long,
Hope feels weak, but we must be strong.
Through storms that rage, through winds that howl,
Hope is the bird that refuses to bow.

In every crack, a sliver of light,
A tiny spark in the deepest night.
It whispers softly, "Hold on tight,"
"Morning comes, no matter the plight."

With each small step, the path grows clear,
Hope finds a way to draw us near.
In adversity, we find our might,
With hope as our guide, we rise to new heights.

Silent Echoes

In rooms so quiet, where we once laughed,
Your whispers linger, like a soft draft.
Memories float like leaves in the breeze,
Reminding me of our shared stories.

The chairs are empty, the air feels still,
Missing the warmth that used to fill.
Though losing you brings tears and pain,
In my heart, your love remains.

Each morning brings your memory near,
In the starry skies, you still appear.
Though grief walks with me, side by side,
In these silent echoes, you abide.

In the Heartbeat of the City

In the city's ceaseless heartbeat,
Rush-hour rivers, streaming lights—
Every soul in swift pursuit,
Chasing dreams through sleepless nights.

Skyscrapers stretch to touch the stars,
Taxicabs in yellow swarms,
Coffee steams in hurried hands,
Life unfolds in buzzing forms.

Yet, amidst this loud ballet,
Silence finds its subtle seat—
In the park where old trees whisper,
And shadowed benches offer retreat.

A solitary figure pauses,
Away from the neon glow,
Finding peace in quiet corners,
Where time moves soft and slow.

Reflections ripple in a puddle,
A mirror to the racing minds,
In stillness, hearts confront their hopes,
In stillness, what's lost, one finds.

Underneath the urban roar,
Lies a silence deep and vast,
Holding space for weary spirits,
In moments that quietly last.

For in the rush we overlook,
What only stillness can bestow:
The beauty of a fleeting thought,
The city's heart—a gentle echo.

"Beyond the Screen: Rediscovering Connection"

Screens light up, we look away,
Lost in digital worlds that sway.
Tech connects us, mile to mile,
But misses the warmth of a smile.

We talk, we text, fast and free,
But touch and presence just can't be.
Screens build walls we can't see through,
Missing real moments, old and new.

Let's pause the scroll, the endless tap,
Find time for a handshake, a hug, a clap.
Tech is a tool, not a chain,
Use it wisely, let true connections remain.

Pen is mightier than the sword

In the poet's gentle grasp,
Lies a tool, mightier than any clasp.
Not of iron, sharp and cold,
But of ink, bold stories told.

A sword can cut, bring a sudden end,
But a pen can heal, can mend.
It writes of love, of peace, of pain,
Bringing wisdom, like gentle rain.

In words, there's power to overcome fear,
To fight the battles far and near.
A simple pen, in steady hands,

Can move the heart, can change the lands.

So here's to the pen, mightier than the blade,
Crafting worlds that never fade.
A quiet force, strong and true,
In each line, the world anew.

Chasing Tomorrow

In the quiet corners of our hearts,
Dreams stir, ready to start.
Aspirations like stars in the night,
Guiding us with their gentle light.

We reach for the sky, so vast and blue,
Hoping to make our dreams come true.
Every step, every try,
Builds the path where our hopes lie.

Through challenges, through fears,
Through the flow of relentless tears,
Our dreams push us to explore,
To strive, to seek, to find much more.

With every sunrise, hope renews,
Filling our days with vibrant hues.
For in our dreams, we find the strength,
To go to any length.

So let us dream, let us aspire,
To reach beyond, to climb higher.
In dreams, our hearts find their wings,
In aspirations, our spirit sings.

Wisdom's Gift

In the twilight of years, wisdom whispers,
Tales of times, of smiles and whispers.
With every wrinkle, a story told,
Of youthful springs and winters cold.

Eyes that sparkle with knowing grace,
Glimpses of the life they've traced.
Hands that hold the world so tight,
Gentle now, in the fading light.

Lessons learned from each fall and rise,
Shared under the vast, endless skies.
Words like treasures, freely given,
Life's mysteries, slowly riven.

For wisdom comes not from books alone,
But from the heart's every beat and tone.
A journey through the maze of years,
Finding joy, overcoming fears.

So let us listen, let us learn,
From those who wait for their last turn.
For in their tales, we find the key,
To live our lives, rich and free.